W9-CHA-058

Derek Jeter
Champion
Baseball
Star

Ken Rappoport

E **Enslow Publishers, Inc.**
40 Industrial Road
Box 398
Berkeley Heights, NJ 07922
USA

http://www.enslow.com

Original edition published as *Super Sports Star Derek Jeter* in 2004.

Library of Congress Cataloging-in-Publication Data

Rappoport, Ken.
 Derek Jeter : champion baseball star / Ken Rappoport.
   p. cm. — (Sports star champions)
 Includes index.
 Summary: "Discusses the life of New York Yankees shortstop Derek Jeter, including his childhood and minor-league
career, individual highlights from his major-league career, and his championship seasons with the Yankees"—Provided
by publisher.
 ISBN 978-0-7660-4025-0
 1. Jeter, Derek, 1974-—Juvenile literature. 2. Baseball players—United States—Biography—Juvenile literature.
I. Title.
 GV865.J48R38 2013
 796.357092—dc23
 [B]
                          2011033514
Future editions:
Paperback ISBN 978-1-4644-0159-6
ePUB ISBN 978-1-4645-1066-3
PDF ISBN 978-1-4646-1066-0

032012 Lake Book Manufacturing, Inc., Melrose Park, IL

Printed in the United States of America

10 9 8 7 6 5 4 3 2 1

To Our Readers: We have done our best to make sure all Internet addresses in this book were active and appropriate
when we went to press. However, the author and the publisher have no control over and assume no liability for the material
available on those Internet sites or on other Web sites they may link to. Any comments or suggestions can be sent by e-mail
to comments@enslow.com or to the address on the back cover.

♲ Enslow Publishers, Inc., is committed to printing our books on recycled paper. The paper in every book contains 10% to
30% post-consumer waste (PCW). The cover board on the outside of each book contains 100% PCW. Our goal is to do our
part to help young people and the environment too!

Illustration Credits: AP Images / Bill Kostroun, pp. 1, 5, 6, 14, 18, 32, 42; AP Images / David J. Phillip, p. 41; AP Images
/ Frank Franklin II, pp. 8, 10; AP Images / Julie Jacobson, p. 16; AP Images / Kathy Kmonicek, p. 4; AP Images / Kathy
Willens, pp. 13, 28; AP Images / Louis Requena, p. 22; AP Images / Mark Lennihan, pp. 26, 36; AP Images / Mark J. Terrill,
p. 34; AP Images / Mel Evans, p. 24; AP Images / Reed Saxon, p. 38; AP Images / Richard Harbus, p. 20; AP Images / Ron
Kuntz, p. 30.

Cover Illustration: AP Images / Bill Kostroun (Derek Jeter).

Contents

Introduction

Just call him the "Captain." When talking about the New York Yankees, that can only mean one player: Derek Jeter.

As the leader of the Yankees, Jeter commands respect and admiration as few other players in Major League Baseball. The Yankees shortstop has been at the center of all the team's successes since 1996.

He jumped to the top in his first season as the Yankees shortstop. In 1996, he helped the Yankees win their first World Series in eighteen years. By the age of twenty-six, he had already won four World Series titles.

His clutch play, especially in the postseason, has been second to none on the team. He always seems to get the key hit or make the key play at the right time.

Derek Jeter is the New York Yankees' captain. He has helped lead the Yankees to win multiple World Series championships.

Jeter means more to the Yankees than just cold statistics. Ask any opponent who has watched the hard-working Yankees captain rise to the occasion time after time. Or, better yet, ask his teammates who see him perform baseball miracles every day.

"Forty, 50, 60 years from now, fans are going to read the back of his baseball card and see a lot of hits," teammate Alex Rodriguez said. "That's pretty amazing, but that won't capture even 50 percent of it."

Derek Jeter has been playing shortstop for the Yankees since his rookie season in 1996. He has become one of the all-time great players in Yankees history.

Derek Jeter at bat during the game against the Tampa Bay Rays in which he tied Lou Gehrig for the most hits by a Yankee.

Chasing
Lou Gehrig

It was late in the 2009 season. Derek Jeter was about to make history.

He needed just four hits to pass Lou Gehrig on the all-time New York Yankees' hits list. An expectant crowd of 45,848 showed up at Yankee Stadium in hopes of seeing Jeter break the team record set by the most durable player in Yankees history.

Jeter had gone twelve straight at bats without a hit. But now, Jeter's bat suddenly came alive. The Yankees captain exploded for three hits to tie Gehrig with 2,721.

Derek Jeter smacks a single in the third inning against the Baltimore Orioles on September 11, 2009, to pass Lou Gehrig as the Yankees all-time hits leader.

"It was kind of mind-boggling to know my name is next to his," Jeter said of the Yankee great known as The Iron Horse, because of his record consecutive-game streak.

Everyone was standing and applauding when Jeter tied Gehrig with a single in the seventh inning. That not only included Yankees fans, but the opposing Tampa Bay Rays as well. Jeter's parents were among the fans enjoying their son's performance.

Two days later, Jeter had a chance to break the record. The Baltimore Orioles were in town on a chilly, rainy night.

Facing the Orioles' Chris Tillman, Jeter ripped a single past first baseman Luke Scott into right field. Hit number 2,722 was in the books—a Yankees record!

Jeter's historic hit triggered a rush of teammates from the dugout. They surrounded him at first base as the fans continued to cheer and applaud. They had sat through an hour-and-a-half rain delay and more steady rain to see the Captain make history.

"It wasn't ideal conditions tonight for the fans to stick around," Jeter said. "It really means a lot. They've been here since Day 1 and they've always been supportive."

Derek Jeter celebrates with teammates after breaking the all-time Yankees hits record.

Jeter singled again his next time up, putting himself two hits ahead of Gehrig before leaving the game in the second rain delay.

"He's part of Yankee history now," Orioles manager Dave Trembley said. "He has the most hits ever for that franchise. He has always represented himself and that organization with class, and he deserves it."

CHAPTER TWO

Born to Be a Yankee

As a young boy, it was Derek Jeter's dream to play shortstop for the Yankees.

Derek woke up early to play baseball every day. "All his cousins would be sleeping, and he would say, 'C'mon, Gram, let's throw,'" his grandmother said. "He wanted to be a pitcher then. I was his catcher. Even as a little kid his throw would knock me over."

Derek's grandmother loved the Yankees. She took him to games. Before long, he was a big fan. His blue Yankees windbreaker was his favorite jacket. He also owned a gold Yankees medallion. His favorite player was Dave Winfield. Someday, he hoped to be just like his hero.

"Kids I went to school with used to laugh when I told them I wanted to play major league baseball," Derek said. "People said that no one from Kalamazoo had played in the majors, so I couldn't do it."

But while growing up in the Michigan town, Derek thought otherwise. Derek's father gave him baseball lessons. Charles Jeter was a baseball player himself in college. "I practiced at it every day," Jeter said. "As far as I can remember, I was always in baseball."

Very often that meant playing with his sister, Sharlee, and mother, Dot. "My mom and sister would be in the outfield and would flag down all the balls I would hit," Jeter said.

In Little League, Derek played three infield positions. He was a shortstop, second baseman, and third baseman.

UP CLOSE!

Other than baseball, Derek's favorite sport to play and watch is basketball.

Derek Jeter jumps to make a throw during infield practice before a spring training game. When Derek told kids at school that he wanted to play major-league baseball, they laughed at him. But that never stopped him from practicing every day.

In Little League, Derek Jeter played three infield positions. He eventually chose shortstop and became one of the best in the major leagues.

His father coached him. Derek learned from both his parents to work hard and respect others.

Derek was born in Pequannock, New Jersey, on June 26, 1974. His father is black and from Alabama. His mother is white and from New Jersey. When Derek was four, the family moved to Kalamazoo, Michigan. His father had a job there as a school counselor. But Derek liked to spend his summers in New Jersey with his grandmother. He went to games at Yankee Stadium. He played baseball from dawn to dusk.

A view of the new Yankee Stadium shortly after it opened in April 2009. Derek Jeter liked to spend the summers at his grandmother's house in New Jersey. During that time, he often went to Yankee Stadium to watch the Yankees play.

Turning Pro

In high school, Derek was the hardest worker on his team. "He was the last one off the field every night," coach Don Zomer said. "He loves the game of baseball."

A buzz went through the crowd as the high-school team took the field. The stands were packed. Everyone was there to see Derek Jeter. In his senior year in high school, he was the star attraction.

Several major-league scouts were watching. They came from all over the country to see Derek play. And they were amazed.

"Even his outs were impressive," Zomer said. "Derek hit balls normal high school players just couldn't handle."

Derek Jeter's sweet swing helped him win many national awards following an amazing baseball season in his senior year of high school.

In his senior year, he led his team with a .508 batting average. That means he had at least one hit every two times at the plate.

Derek was named the National High School Player of the Year in 1992. He was not only tops in baseball. He was also among the top students in his class. Derek was an honor student with a 3.82 grade average.

He accepted a baseball scholarship from the University of Michigan. Then he waited to see what happened in the baseball draft. Teams take turns picking the best players out of high school and college. Derek hoped to be picked by his favorite team, the New York Yankees.

UP CLOSE!

In 1992, Derek Jeter was named Gatorade High School Athlete of the Year, *USA Today* High School Baseball Player of the Year, and American Baseball Coaches Association High School Player of the Year.

The New York Yankees drafted Derek Jeter in 1992. He was the first high school player to be selected by a major-league team that year. In this photo, Jeter (left) compares gloves with fellow Yankees Jim Leyritz (center) and Mike Gallego prior to a game on September 12, 1992. Eighteen-year-old Jeter had just completed high school in June.

On draft day, the phone rang in Derek's house. He held his breath. It was the Yankees. They had selected him in the first round of the draft. He was the first high school player picked by a major-league team. Derek was thrilled, but he also wanted to play college ball. The Yankees helped make up his mind.

"Education is a big thing in our family," Derek said later. "Signing with the Yankees was no easy decision because I really wanted to go to school and play baseball at Michigan. But I couldn't say no when they were paying for college, too."

Derek picked up a seven-hundred-thousand-dollar bonus just for signing a contract. He was only eighteen years old and heading for pro ball. But there were some hard times ahead for him.

Derek Jeter jumps to turn a double play during his rookie season for the Yankees. As a young player straight out of high school, Jeter had a lot to learn before he would achieve success at the major-league level.

Up the Ladder

Derek Jeter was not hitting. He was making errors. He was playing in the Gulf Coast rookie league in Tampa, Florida. He was far from home and missed his friends and family. He was very unhappy.

"That first year was rough," Jeter said. "That was the first time I was ever away from home, and I was terrible. Two and a half months seemed like forever to me." Jeter thought he had made a mistake by signing with the Yankees. "You start thinking, 'Were you ready? Should you have gone to college?'"

Derek Jeter sprints up the first-base line after hitting a single during a minor-league rehab start for the Trenton Thunder on July 2, 2011. This stint in the minors was to help him recover from a leg injury during the 2011 season. In his first minor-league season with the Yankees, Jeter struggled and was homesick.

Next stop for Jeter: the Greensboro Hornets. The Hornets played in the South Atlantic League. It was the first step up from the rookie league. But it was still a long way from the major leagues.

At Greensboro, Jeter improved his batting. However, he was still having trouble in the field. He made error after error at shortstop. That was not the only thing that was bothering him.

"I was homesick," Jeter said. "When they told me at Tampa that I was coming [to Greensboro], I should have been happy to move up. But I just wanted to go home."

In 1993, Jeter made 56 errors, the second highest by a shortstop in his league. Jeter was not discouraged, though. He told himself: Work harder. His defense improved, so

UP CLOSE!

When he first came to New York to play for the Yankees, Derek was nicknamed "The Kid" by sports writers. He was only twenty years old.

Derek Jeter poses on the dugout steps at Yankee Stadium on September 14, 1994, with his *Baseball America's* Minor League Player of the Year trophy.

much so that one national baseball magazine named Jeter its best minor-league defensive shortstop. By the time he was promoted to Columbus, the Yankees' highest farm team, Jeter was named 1994 Minor League Player of the Year by several publications.

He was ready to join the parent club in New York. "I went out on the field and looked around and it was like, 'Am I really here?'" Jeter said of the first time he walked into Yankee Stadium as a regular with the Yankees.

It was the summer of 1995. Yankees shortstop Tony Fernandez was hurt. The Yankees brought Jeter up from the minors. He played fifteen games.

In 1996, Jeter was named starting shortstop for the Yankees on Opening Day. Jeter was nervous. He knew it would not be easy. New York baseball fans demanded the best from their players.

Jeter got off to a good start. In his first game, he hit a home run against Cleveland. The Yankees beat the Indians, 7–1. Jeter did not let up. By the end of the season, he had a solid .314 batting average. He scored 104 runs and drove in 78 runs. He sparked the Yankees into the playoffs.

In the postseason, he continued to hit the ball very hard. His .412 batting average helped the Yankees knock out

Derek Jeter had a tremendous regular season as a rookie in 1996 and continued his success in the postseason. In this photo, Jeter scores the winning run in the twelfth inning of the Yankees divisional playoff game against the Texas Rangers on October 2, 1996.

Texas in the first round. Then the battle for the American League title opened in New York. The Yankees faced Baltimore. They hoped to get the jump on the Orioles at home. Baltimore was leading, 4–3, in the eighth inning when Jeter came up to hit.

He hit a long drive to right field. Home run! The score was tied. Then in the eleventh inning, Bernie Williams homered. The Yankees won, 5–4. The Yankees kept winning. Jeter provided the spark with a key homer and a .417 batting average against the Orioles.

World Series time. The Yankees faced the Atlanta Braves. The Braves won the first two games in New York. Things looked bad for the Yankees. The Series moved to Atlanta. The Yankees needed to win at least two of the three games to have a chance. They won all three. Now the teams were back at Yankee Stadium. The Yankees could clinch the Series in Game 6. Jeter drove in a run. His hit sparked a three-run rally. The Yankees beat the Braves, 3–2. It was their first world championship since 1978.

Derek Jeter was later given another prize. He was named Rookie of the Year.

"It was just an incredible year," Jeter said.

Derek Jeter won the Rookie of the Year award and a World Series title in his first full season with the Yankees. Jeter would achieve much individual and team success at the beginning of his career.

Rising to the Occasion

Derek Jeter was worried. It was the 1997 season, and there was trouble. He was striking out. His batting average had dropped.

"I've made a lot of mistakes," he said during the year. "Part of the problem is that I'm trying to prove last year wasn't a fluke, and I try too hard."

The season ended too quickly for Jeter and the Yankees. They were knocked out of the playoffs. They missed their chance to become world champions again.

Could they make a comeback in 1998? The Yankees came to spring training camp with just that goal in mind. They worked hard. They were going to show the baseball world that they were the best team.

Derek Jeter throws to first base during a game against the Detroit Tigers on July 22, 1998. Jeter helped lead the Yankees to an amazing 114 wins during the 1998 regular season.

By May, the Yankees were in first place. On May 18, they had the top record in baseball at 28–9. It was the best start by a Yankees team since 1928. Jeter was hot. He was hitting .337. That was one of the best batting averages in the league. He paced the Yankees with ten steals.

Day by day, the victories piled up. When the regular season ended, the Yankees had won an amazing 114 games. It was the best record in American League history. Jeter played a big role. He nearly doubled his home run total of the previous season. He boosted his batting average and RBIs to career bests. The Yankees were back in the playoffs for the third straight year.

No less than a World Series title would satisfy them. They rolled through the postseason. In the World Series, the Yankees met the San Diego Padres. They opened with two victories at Yankee Stadium. They flew west to play the next two games in San Diego. The Yankees added another victory in Game 3. New York was one win away from the world championship.

A crowd of 65,427 filled Qualcomm Stadium in San Diego. The fans saw a great pitchers' duel. It was the Yankees' Andy Pettitte against the Padres' Kevin Brown. After five innings, the teams were scoreless.

Derek Jeter slides into home to score a run during Game 4 of the World Series on October 21, 1998. Jeter's dash to home plate started a rally for the Yankees, clinching their World Series championship.

Then in the sixth inning, Jeter beat out an infield hit. Paul O'Neill followed with a double sending Jeter to third. Bernie Williams hit a chopper to the mound. Jeter got a good jump and raced home for the game's first run. It was the start of a three-run rally. The Yankees were on their way to a 3–0 victory. They became world champions again.

What a season for the Yankees and Derek Jeter. The Yankees won 125 games counting the regular season and playoffs. That was more than any team in baseball history. They had made their case as the best team ever. And Jeter had made his case as one of baseball's best players.

Derek Jeter won four World Series titles in the first five years of his career with the Yankees. In this photo, Jeter celebrates a Game 4 victory during the 2000 Series against the New York Mets.

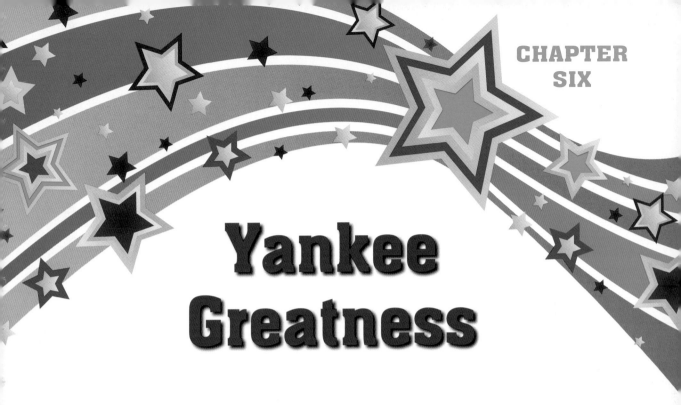

Yankee Greatness

It was getting to be a habit for the Yankees: Another year, another visit to the World Series.

It was 1999. Jeter had just finished his greatest regular season. He batted .349 with 24 home runs. He scored 134 runs and drove in 102. In the playoffs, he hit safely in every game. He helped the Yankees beat Atlanta for the title.

Jeter showed he was a player who thrived under great pressure. He extended his postseason hitting streak to seventeen games. It was a major-league record. "If this is a dream, don't wake me up," Jeter said.

Derek Jeter takes a big swing during a second-round game of the World Baseball Classic on March 13, 2006. Jeter started at shortstop for Team USA in 2006 and 2009.

Were there more titles to come? The New York Mets had other ideas. As champions of the National League, they faced the American League champion Yankees in the 2000 World Series. The so-called "Subway Series" sparked excitement all over New York. It was the first time the Mets and Yankees had met in the World Series.

After three games, the Yankees held a 2–1 lead. Each game was a thriller. At Shea Stadium for Game 4, the Mets could have tied the Series with a win. Jeter stepped into the batter's box to lead off. He lashed the first pitch. Home run! In his next at bat, he tripled and then he scored. The Yankees were off to a 3–2 victory.

On the following night, the Yankees fell behind the Mets. But Jeter hit a home run. Tie game! The shot sparked the Yankees to a 4–2 victory and another world championship—the Yankees' fourth in five years. During the season, Jeter had been the Most Valuable Player at the All-Star Game. Now he was also the World Series MVP. No other player had ever done that.

Another honor for Jeter: He was named starting shortstop for Team USA at the World Baseball Classic in 2006 and 2009. During those years, he also broke Luis Aparicio's record for most hits by a shortstop in major-league history.

That was fine with Jeter, but he had a more important goal: return to another World Series with the Yankees.

Since beating the Mets in the 2000 World Series, the Yankees had gone eight years without winning the title. After winning four championships in five years, Jeter and his Yankee teammates were frustrated. Would they ever get back to the World Series?

Finally in 2009, the Yankees made their return to the top. They faced the Philadelphia Phillies, who were gunning for their second straight world title. Led by Jeter, the Yankees won three of the first five games. They returned to the Bronx for Game 6, needing only one victory to close out the Series.

Jeter singled twice, doubled, and scored twice to lead the Yankees to a 7–3 victory. After a nine-year wait, the Yankees had finally won their record twenty-seventh world championship.

The Captain had shown the way. Jeter hit safely in every game for a championship-caliber .407 batting average. His eleven hits were only one short of the record in a six-game World Series.

"You forget how good it feels," Jeter said. "(The titles) are all meaningful, but this one here is special because it's been a long, long time."

Derek Jeter smashes a ground rule double to center field during Game 6 of the World Series on November 4, 2009. Jeter went 3 for 5 in the game and scored two runs. The Yankees' victory over the Philadelphia Phillies was Jeter's fifth championship.

Derek Jeter watches his home run sail over the fence for his 3,000th career hit while his teammates celebrate in the dugout behind him. Jeter was the first player to reach 3,000 hits while wearing Yankee pinstripes.

Jeter, playing under a new three-year contract that earned him more than $50 million, was on his way to breaking Lou Gehrig's team record for hits. There was one other mark Jeter had his eye on: 3,000 career hits. Only twenty-seven players in major-league history were part of the "3,000 Hit Club."

But, not so fast. Jeter's quest for 3,000 hits was delayed in June 2011, when he suffered an injury to his right calf. He was placed on the disabled list. He missed eighteen games. He returned to action in early July still needing six hits to reach the 3,000-hit plateau.

Three hits in Cleveland moved Jeter within three of the mark. Jeter returned to Yankee Stadium where a sellout crowd awaited the Yankees and their popular captain. Jeter picked up a double against the Tampa Bay Rays for career hit 2,998. Only two more for 3,000.

After a rainout sent the disappointed fans home on Friday night, July 8, the next day belonged to the Yankees' All-Star shortstop. He singled for hit number 2,999 in the first inning. Then in the third, he worked the count to 3–2 against the Rays' David Price before fouling off a pitch. He slammed the next pitch over the wall in left-center field for his third home run of the season.

Welcome to the 3,000 Hit Club, Derek Jeter!

Jeter was mobbed by teammates as he crossed home plate. Yankees fans were on their feet, celebrating their hometown hero.

Jeter was hardly finished. He smashed three more hits to give him a perfect 5 for 5 for the day, including the game-winning single as the Yankees beat the Rays, 5–4.

"Hitting a home run is the last thing I thought about," Jeter said. "I just wanted to hit the ball hard."

Yankees manager Joe Girardi said of Jeter's historic accomplishment, "Wow, he really knows how to do it. This is a guy who has always been a big-time player in a big moment."

As a boy, Derek Jeter had dreamed of playing for the Yankees. He idolized all the Yankees players, especially Dave Winfield. And now he could count himself among the all-time Yankees greats.

Career Statistics

BATTING REGULAR SEASON CAREER STATS

YEAR	TEAM	G	AB	R	H	2B	3B	HR	RBI	BB	SO	SB	AVG
1995	NYY	15	48	5	12	4	1	0	7	3	11	0	.250
1996	NYY	157	582	104	183	25	6	10	78	48	102	14	.314
1997	NYY	159	654	116	190	31	7	10	70	74	125	23	.291
1998	NYY	149	626	127	203	25	8	19	84	57	119	30	.324
1999	NYY	158	627	134	219	37	9	24	102	91	116	19	.349
2000	NYY	148	593	119	201	31	4	15	73	68	99	22	.339
2001	NYY	150	614	110	191	35	3	21	74	56	99	27	.311
2002	NYY	157	644	124	191	26	0	18	75	73	114	32	.297
2003	NYY	119	482	87	156	25	3	10	52	43	88	11	.324
2004	NYY	154	643	111	188	44	1	23	78	46	99	23	.292
2005	NYY	159	654	122	202	25	5	19	70	77	117	14	.309
2006	NYY	154	623	118	214	39	3	14	97	69	102	34	.343
2007	NYY	156	639	102	206	39	4	12	73	56	100	15	.322
2008	NYY	150	596	88	179	25	3	11	69	52	85	11	.300
2009	NYY	153	634	107	212	27	1	18	66	72	90	30	.334
2010	NYY	157	663	111	179	30	3	10	67	63	106	18	.270
2011	NYY	131	546	84	162	24	4	6	61	46	81	16	.297
CAREER		2,426	9,868	1,769	3,088	492	65	240	1,196	994	1,653	339	.313

G–Games played
AB.–At bats
R–Runs

H–Hits
2B–Doubles
3B–Triples

HR.–Home runs
RBI–Runs batted in
BB.–Walks

SO–Strikeouts
SB–Stolen bases
AVG–Batting average

Where to Write to Derek Jeter

Mr. Derek Jeter
c/o The New York Yankees
Yankee Stadium
1 East 161st Street
Bronx, NY 10451

Glossary

All-Star Game—The midsummer classic matches the best players in the American and National leagues.

major leagues—The top professional league in baseball. The majors include the American and National leagues.

minor leagues—The minors are made up of all the other professional leagues. The players hope to some day play in the major leagues.

Most Valuable Player (MVP)—The award is given each year to the best player in the league. It is also handed out to the best player in the annual All-Star Game.

rookie—A player in his first full season in professional sports.

scholarship—An award that allows a student to attend college for free.

shortstop—Part of the "middle infield" with the second baseman. The shortstop usually has the best range and strongest arm of all the infielders.

World Series—Each fall, the champions of the American and National leagues battle for the World Series title.

Further Reading

Books

Bednar, Chuck. *Derek Jeter: All-Star Major League Baseball Player.* Broomall, Pa.: Mason Crest Publishers, 2010.

Donovan, Sandy. *Derek Jeter.* Minneapolis, Minn.: Lerner Publications Company, 2011.

Greenberg, Keith Elliot. *Derek Jeter: Spectacular Shortstop.* Minneapolis, Minn.: Twenty-First Century Books, 2011.

Howell, Brian. *Derek Jeter: Yankee Great.* Edina, Minn.: ABDO Publishing Company, 2011.

Mills, Clifford W. *Derek Jeter.* New York: Chelsea House, 2007.

Internet Addresses

Baseball-Reference.com: Derek Jeter
<http://www.baseball-reference.com/players/j/jeterde01.shtml>

ESPN: Derek Jeter Stats, News, Pictures, Bio, and Videos
<http://espn.go.com/mlb/player/_/id/3246/derek-jeter>

The Official Site of the New York Yankees
<http://newyork.yankees.mlb.com/index.jsp?c_id=nyy>

Index

A
all-time hits record, 7–10, 39, 43–44
Atlanta Braves, 29, 37
awards, honors, 19, 27, 29, 39

B
Baltimore Orioles, 9, 29
baseball career
  bonuses, 21
  errors, mistakes, 23, 25, 31
  high-school, 17–19
  Little League, 12–15
  minor league, 23–27
  practice habits, 11–12, 15
  scholarships, 19
batting average, 27, 29, 33, 37
Brown, Kevin, 35

C
clutch play, 4

F
Fernandez, Tony, 27

G
Gehrig, Lou, 7, 9

Greensboro Hornets, 25–27

J
Jeter, Charles, 9, 12, 15
Jeter, Derek
  childhood, family life, 15
  overview, 4–5
  salary, 21, 43
Jeter, Dot, 9, 12, 15

M
Minor League Player of the Year 1994, 27

N
National High School Player of the Year, 1992, 19
New York Mets, 39
New York Yankees
  American League title 1996, 29
  drafting of Jeter by, 21
  records, 33, 35
  season 1996, 27
  season 1997, 31
  season 1998, 31–33
  season 1999, 37
  season 2000, 39
  World Series 1996, 29

  World Series 1998, 33–35
  World Series 2000, 39
  World Series 2009, 40

O
O'Neill, Paul, 35

P
Pettitte, Andy, 35
Philadelphia Phillies, 40

R
records, breaking, 7–10, 39, 43–44
Rookie of the Year 1996, 29

S
San Diego Padres, 33–35
Subway Series, 39

T
Tampa Bay Rays, 9, 43–44
Team USA, 39
Tillman, Chris, 9

W
Williams, Bernie, 29, 35
Winfield, Dave, 11, 44
World Series MVP, 39